MONSTER POETRY

LONDON

Edited By Elle Berry

First published in Great Britain in 2018 by:

Young Writers
Remus House
Coltsfoot Drive
Peterborough
PE2 9BF
Telephone: 01733 890066
Website: www.youngwriters.co.uk

All Rights Reserved
Book Design by Ben Reeves
© Copyright Contributors 2018
SB ISBN 978-1-78896-835-5
Printed and bound in the UK by BookPrintingUK
Website: www.bookprintinguk.com
YB0378X

FOREWORD

Young Writers was created in 1991 with the express purpose of promoting and encouraging creative writing. Each competition we create is tailored to the relevant age group, hopefully giving each child the inspiration and incentive to create their own piece of writing, whether it's a poem or a short story. We truly believe that seeing it in print gives pupils a sense of achievement and pride in their work and themselves.

Our latest competition, Monster Poetry, focuses on uncovering the different techniques used in poetry and encouraging pupils to explore new ways to write a poem. Using a mix of imagination, expression and poetic styles, this anthology is an impressive snapshot of the inventive, original and skilful writing of young people today. These poems showcase the creativity and talent of these budding new writers as they learn the skills of writing, and we hope you are as entertained by them as we are.

CONTENTS

Independent Entries

Lily Razok (8)	1
Theo Marsh (11)	2

Argyle Primary School

Maeda Mohamed (8)	3
Ibrahim Hossain (8)	4
Sahibah Zaman (9)	5
Fatheha Ahmed (8)	6
Sayyeda Badran (10)	7

Ecole Jeannine Manuel

Andreas Stein (10)	8
Margot Paré (10)	9
Antoine Bacuvier (11)	10
Emile De Margerie (10)	11

Eveline Day School

William Coney (8)	12
Stanley Taylor (8)	14
Esme Freeman (9)	15
Arlo Bowles (8)	16
Isabella Thornton (8)	18
Paul Kronacker (9)	20
Mischa Jayaram (9)	21
Jasmine Tafader (7)	22
Jack McBride (8)	23

Gallions Mount Primary School

Omoseye Badejo (9)	24
Opemipo Enigbokan (9)	25

Lathom Junior School

Kapirna Pirapakaran (8)	26
Kavanjot Kaur Lall (8)	28
Aqsa Ahmad (8)	29
Ashia Hassan Dhinbil aden (7)	30
Zara Waqar Bhatti (8)	31
Amaara Sana Jabar (7)	32
Maheen Saqib (8)	33

Marvels Lane Primary School

Dillani Arulananthan (10)	34
Eris Gyan (11)	36
Chelsea Amankwah (11)	38
Teigan Stuart (11)	40
Rupertas Brazdzius (11)	41
Jathursa Satkunarasa (11)	42
Ariana Ioana Popovici (11)	44
Salvijus Brazdzius (9)	45
Jennifer Wang (10)	46

Mitchell Brook Primary School

Farhiya Hassan (10)	47
Carina Carter (6)	48

Notre Dame Catholic Primary School

Namitha Lakshmikantham Arava (9)	49
Valina John (9)	50
Chara Ibeauuchi (9)	51
Jedi Olaose (9)	52

Rosemary Works School

Edith Christie (9)	53
Eleanor Stewart	54
Sam Maguire (9)	56
Oliver Altan Bulus (9)	57

St Bernadette RC Junior School

Maja Agnieszka Lockwood (10)	58
Tia Scott-Lewis (10)	60
Yesheemah Constantine	62
Jahzae Barnes (9)	64
Anastasia Peters Macauley (7)	66
Samantha Motato (10)	67
Tahirah Heron (10)	68
Isabella Quintero (9)	70
Jotham Osorio (9)	72
Evelyn Romo Vosas (10)	73
Melissa Ocampo (10)	74
Yamrot Legesse Daniel (10)	75
Antwarn Philippe-Watson (10)	76
Ciara Murphy (10)	77
Noel Chiagozie Opurum (8)	78
Oliwier Szczekala (10)	79
Samuel Martin Muñoz (8)	80
Megan Murphy (8)	81
Kevin Gryniewicz (10)	82
Max Fernandes (10)	83
Paula Anais Campoverde (8)	84
Admire Goswell (9)	85
Whitney Amankwah Youles (9)	86
Paula Andrea Segura (10)	87
Caleb Michael Asare (10)	88
Daniel Forson Fosu (10)	89
Isabella Pereira (9)	90
Beatriz Ferreira (10)	91
Dionne Boateng (10)	92
Maria Iwan (10)	93
Alexandru Andrei Cirstea (9)	94
Leticia Gouveia (10)	95
Luke Adams (9)	96
Asiâ-Léigh Hayles-Chin (9)	97
Dainah Georgia Dyer (10)	98

Rufta Angosom (9)	99
Ruby Hanson (8)	100

St Chad's RC Primary School

Keno Agbandje (11)	101
Theresa-Mae Brown	102
Michelle Appiah Arhin (8)	105
Ayen Achiri-Ngu (8)	106
Jeffrey Osei-Owusu (9)	108
Adrianna Grace Pope	109
Ethan Czarnecki	110
Mercedes Ohenewah Abiana Agyiri (8)	111

St Mary's & St John's CE School

Tia Simone Thomas (10)	112

St Paul's Way Foundation School

Taneesha Ahmed	114
Khalil Umar (8)	116
Nishat Chowdhury (8)	118
Ishrath Haque (8)	119
Ava Miah	120
Omer Ozturk (8)	122
Ahmad Ismailov (7)	123
Sulaiman Uddin (8)	124
Ahana Zaina (8)	125
Humayra Afsa (8)	126
Shyann Myrie (8)	127
Jannah Kolil Uddin (8)	128
Ismail Hussain	129
Blake Power (7)	130
Miraj Ishraq	131
Daniel Fagbile (8)	132

The Dominie

Edoardo Walker (9)	133
Amber Beauchamp (9)	134
Otto Matthias Ballard (7)	135
Sara Sonmez de Paz (7)	136
Nanna Marie Olsen (9)	137

Malachi Nunoo-Menash (9)	138
Monty Fisher (9)	139
Rafer Smith (8)	140
Taylor Caine-Hall (9)	141
Rory Fitzsimons (7)	142
Harry Deacon (8)	143
Alexander Hayes (7)	144
Daniel Petrovic (9)	145
Oscar Doernte (7)	146
Elina Eva Brown (9)	147
Vincent Martini Fitzgerald (8)	148

Thomas's Kensington

Olivia Bentley (10)	149

Tiverton Primary School

Luqman Ibrahim (10)	150

THE POEMS

My Adorable Monster

When I came from a massive port
I saw a monster, cute and short
She had adorable, pretty eyes
And guess what? She knew how to fly
She had fluffy, soft ears
Plus she had shiny diamond tears
She had a rainbow tiny horn
If you knew, she loved popcorn
She can fart out mysterious rainbows
It had a small little bow
We went to unicorn land
And we played in glittery pink sand
She was made out of a cloud
But she never liked to be in a crowd
Her best friend was called Fluffy Cuddle
Who was always in a muddle
We went to space to Glitter World
And the universe was filled with swirls
She had cute violet wings
And she really liked to sing
Finally, her name was Furble Unicorn Glitter.

Lily Razok (8)

Zorg

I met him in an alleyway,
Funny how he ended up that way,
Slouched, curled up in a ball,
Isolated as if he was in a big hall,
He was lonely,
Just lonely.

Until that very day,
He was no one anyway,
But there he was,
People chewed him up and spat him out,
They thought he would definitely shout,
I unlocked the door,
He didn't moan,
All he said was, "I'm home."

Theo Marsh (11)

Deep Inside

There lived a vicious monster named Phoenix.
His scary claws, his sharp teeth scared everyone in his village.
His eyes were as bold as a neon pen.
A red, bloody colour shone through his eyes.
Whenever he went up to people, he just wanted to say hi.
However, people judged him and saw him as a villain.
He looked very different to everyone.
His unique appearance frightened everyone.
One day a young girl was not so mortified as the other.
She approached him and simply just said hi.
Suddenly a smile grew on his face for the very first time.
This brought joy and happiness into his life.
He went from being the most lonely person to being everyone's best friend.
He was no longer seen as a threat but a cuddly, joyful friend loved by everyone.

Maeda Mohamed (8)
Argyle Primary School

The Dragon

The dragon was born in a fiery cave
It smells like rotten eggs
It is so mean and likes chaos of all kinds
It left the volcano
For an adventure party
It needed to be crazy
And make monsters happy
But it met me on a cliff
I unlocked the monster's hut
It fizzed
When the tide came in
Its fiery, fiery skin
Turned green
It said, "Can I join in?"
Then said, "Hooray, someone's joining in!"
They all played party games
And danced like a volcano.

Ibrahim Hossain (8)
Argyle Primary School

Mysterious Pac-Man Monster

I am a monster named Pac-Man
I have several eyes
That you can't count in time
I am a turquoise-coloured monster
That has a lot of pink dots
My dots go away when I have a bit of lime
Call me anytime, I'll come and change colours
People will be scared when I show my yellow
I come from a mountain named Mount Everest
People call me friendly
But inside I am full of hate
Like a volcano about to erupt
Mwahahaha!

Sahibah Zaman (9)
Argyle Primary School

My Mischievous Monster!

Is my mischievous monster under a table
Or playing with my labels?
Is he in the garden up a tree
Or does he want honey from a bee?
Is my monster eating food
Or wearing my favourite snood?
Is he on my special chair
Or fighting a scary bear?
Is my monster looking in the fridge
Or walking across London Bridge?
Where is my mischievous monster?

Fatheha Ahmed (8)
Argyle Primary School

Can You See Me?

Storm lived in a cave,
He was very brave,
He couldn't save and he knew gravity,
He couldn't go rapidly,
One time he went to the galaxy,
It was a fantasy,
But he was in a reality,
And everyone acted angrily,
Because he had gone,
So if you find Storm,
Don't go on your phone,
Just tell him to go home.

Sayyeda Badran (10)
Argyle Primary School

The Beast

A blood-red sunset hit the village
As they prepared for the night
Only one guard stood at the gates
Of the village that night
Then out of the woods came the demon
His body was a carcass of rotting flesh
His eyes were burning coals that shone with malice
On his head were two great ram horns
That glinted in the moonlight
He perched himself and jumped down
To the village gates
A foolish attempt by the guardsman
Who ran at him with his spear
The beast flicked his hand and ripped off his head
The guardsman crumpled to the floor
But that wasn't the only casualty that night
The beast ripped out carnage and hell
And knocked down houses that crumpled
To the ground, but one house did not
And on the door of the house
Were the numbers six, six, six!

Andreas Stein (10)
Ecole Jeannine Manuel

The Sand Man

A long time ago
The beach wasn't the luxurious place
We think of now.
Back then, it was a nightmare.
All the beaches on Earth
Were haunted by this devil.
If anyone dared to swim
The monster would make
A huge wave to drown them.
If anyone placed a pinkie on the sand
The Sand Man would make a colossal earthquake.
One day, a brave girl decided
That she would do something.
She twirled her lasso, choked the Sand Man
And trapped him in a sandcastle.
You can still hear now, the Sand Man's rage
As he creates an earthquake, trying to escape.

Margot Paré (10)
Ecole Jeannine Manuel

The Humman

The humman was born is a hospital
He was red and hairless
He screamed so loudly
That the ears of the monsters would explode
He smelt a chemical white thing he called 'soap'
He used it to attract his prey
He became nasty and hostile when he took
A substance he called 'broccoli'.

When he evolved
He could become nice or nasty
One day I met him in the street
We became friends
We went on vacation
We played
But then he got killed...
By a real monster,

He was a human.

Antoine Bacuvier (11)
Ecole Jeannine Manuel

The Santafluff

A big monster called Santafluff
Was red like blood
And white like snow
He had a big and fluffy belly

All the years he prepared presents for Christmas
At Christmas he delivered all the presents he made
Only by clicking his fingers

All the humans thought it was Santa Claus
But in reality it was Santafluff
The fluffy monster.

Emile De Margerie (10)
Ecole Jeannine Manuel

Freaky The Friendly Monster

Freaky was a friendly guy
He was born like that, he did not try
But in his world, that was not so
Nice and good they thought, "Oh no!"

They bullied him all day and night
With evil tricks and scares and frights
They called him freaky to be mean
They shot at him with laser beams

Poor Freaky felt so sad and blue
He wondered all day what to do
Freaky hatched a cunning plan
To trap and turn the evil clan

He dug a hole, huge and deep
And filled it with some sweets and treats
The monsters came and saw the food
They all dived in, to grab the loot
But then they realised that they were stuck

They shouted, "We're stuck down here,
With all this muck!"

Freaky came and said, "Hello,
What are you doing, stuck down below?
I could get you out with great ease
If you want my help, you have to say *please!*"

The monsters hated this and they did roar
They'd never had to use manners before!
They tried to clamber up the wall
They rolled back down just like a ball

"Calling me names is just absurd
I'll let you out, just say the magic word
If you promise to be good
I'll let you back out into the neighbourhood."

One of the monsters went down on their knees
He took a deep breath and said... "Please!"
From then on the monsters learned how to
Say please a lot, and even thank you
They even stopped calling Freaky names
And let him join in all the games.

William Coney (8)
Eveline Day School

The Feathered Frenzy

The Feathered Frenzy was born from a star
He had feathers of iron and talons of gold
He sought Earth and landed
He ripped up anything living
He tore up trees like they were blades of grass
Whilst he kicked up buildings, he pushed over cars
And threw people far and wide
He crushed roads as if they were crumpled paper
People ran for their lives
I didn't, I stayed where I was
The Feathered Frenzy screeched out his fury
He told me to run or I'd be sorry
But, I knew his weakness: snow
I rushed to my house and got some freezing snow
I flung it at his metallic feathered head.
I saw the flaky snow explode and heard the monster's shrill screech.
I saw him spread his mighty wings
And retreat back to the star.
I heard the people's ecstatic cheers
And I smiled at them with a broad grin.

Stanley Taylor (8)
Eveline Day School

Marvellous Monster

It is cute, it is fluffy
They are harmless
Although lots of people fear them
They come in all shapes and sizes
Fate always manages to creep up on them
Making the babies into the scariest heroes
And the strong, weak and powerless
In stories they are ugly and vicious
But like most things, they are different
So the thing I'm thinking of is very lonely
Because people believe the stories
But really they are fluffy and cute
And clever and kind
They are among the animals
That have the biggest hearts
They are nearly extinct
But still lurk about
The thing I'm thinking of
Is a monster.

Esme Freeman (9)
Eveline Day School

The Monster Ate My Homework

Monsters they're big, they're fat,
They've got slime for boogers
And bellies that wobble like jelly
Well, that stuff may sound very frightening
But that is like a cute teddy bear
Compared to the one I saw
Because I talked to it
I looked it in the eye
And Mrs Degale, I saw him
On the way to school
So, back to the point
His teeth were as sharp as lion's claws
He had enormous eyes in the front
And back of his head
And he spoke to me
Since I can speak alien
I could translate
"Huhum! I have come to rule your world!"
If you even touched him, you would bleed

And that's why I couldn't write
Oh and did I mention
He had teeth as sharp as a lion?
To put it in a short version
The monster ate my homework!

Arlo Bowles (8)
Eveline Day School

This Monster

This monster comes out suddenly,
It can stay for far too long
This monster makes no sense to me
And it is always wrong

This monster is very dangerous
And spoils things with your friends
This monster can upset people
And it never makes amends

This monster can creep up on you
When someone does really well
This monster comes out of nowhere
Without a warning bell

This monster makes life difficult
And it never makes things right
This monster is no good for you
And can keep you awake at night

This monster can lurk inside you
But we should leave it far behind

This monster is called Jealousy
And we can defeat it by being kind!

Isabella Thornton (8)
Eveline Day School

The Dream!

Last night I dreamed a dream
No ordinary dream, a creepy, weird, scary dream
I dreamt a fluffy, cute, happy looking creature
Was watching me
I dreamt a creature was watching me
With its pink skin and smooth-skinned tail
Its scaly angel wings, that glistened like the moon
A feeling lit inside of me
The monster was scared and lost
So I kept him for me
Huh! I woke up and saw a pink-winged
Tailed monster fly out of my window.

Paul Kronacker (9)
Eveline Day School

The Mystery?

I was lying in my bed, ready to sleep
Suddenly, I saw a dark shadow move
I wouldn't dare to look up
All I saw was a fluffy blue tail
I could hear some wind
The shadow turned around and moved closer
I could now see pink, glittery wings
A purple, fluffy body
It turned around and I could see cute eyes
I couldn't believe what I saw
But it was real
It was a monster!

Mischa Jayaram (9)
Eveline Day School

Me

Smooth, sticky, spotty and stretchy
This is what makes me

The other children call me names
And make fun of me

My heart wishes to have friends
Who accept me for me

One eye, six arms and antennae on my head
"Look at that freak" - this is what they shout at me

I want a friend who is like me
I want to be loved for me
I want to be me.

Jasmine Tafader (7)
Eveline Day School

The Monster

The monster is so big and hairy
All the people think he is scary

His senses are so strong
He can feel when he is doing wrong

But he likes to destroy walls
He likes to jump high and fall

He has many scratches
From throwing houses
Which he catches

Tonight he will leave the woods again
To see if he can find a friend.

Jack McBride (8)
Eveline Day School

The Five-Eyed Dragon - Haikus

Beady five red eyes
Ferocious, frightful loud roar
Seeing everything

Do you want to feel
The scorching, sweltering heat?
Well, don't anger him

Oh, he'll have his way
He will have you for supper
Then take your bones out.

Omoseye Badejo (9)
Gallions Mount Primary School

Shadow Monster

Haiku poetry

Hideous, scary
Approaches you in shadows
Dangerous creature.

Venomous, vicious
Strikes you in the darkest night
Lives are in danger.

Horrible, nasty
Close all your windows and hide
Beware citizens.

Opemipo Enigbokan (9)
Gallions Mount Primary School

Maisie Monster's Mission

The creepy monsters crawled inside a book
Which was written by a cook
The main monster was Maisie
Who really loved daisies
She went in first
Because she didn't want to get hurt
As soon as Maisie went in
Someone snapped the book
Her four feet shivered
She was as frightened as a mouse
Her body turned red
Her friends were as worried as she was
They ran away
So the same thing wouldn't happen to them
Later someone super suspicious opened it
Maisie came out and then saw none of her friends
She decided to set a mission to find her furious friends
She went all over the world searching
She destroyed all the homeless houses
And at last she found them

And the moshy monsters went back
To how they were before.

Kapirna Pirapakaran (8)
Lathom Junior School

Fred's Adventures

Once there was a cyclops, Fred.
His friend's names were Edd, Mez and Tedd.
They would play all day in the trenches far away.
Once his friends did not come out to play.
Fred thought, *oh no, what will I do all day?*
Fred thought hard and fast,
And then decided at last,
He wanted to head up to a volcano,
And discover what was inside.
When he got up to the volcano,
He gasped in delight.
There was a creature who looked a lot like Fred.
Fred and the creature became good friends.
They would play all day in the molten hot lava,
And come back home happily to see,
The rest of their friends, and play,
In the trench for the rest of the day.

Kavanjot Kaur Lall (8)
Lathom Junior School

Happy Monster

This is a monster you have never seen
Ever in your life
His name is Scary, he is not mean
But he has five eyes
A big mouth and is a shape-shifter
He's a little cuckoo in the head
But he is invisible and fluffy
He left the house for some reason
To prove to everyone he was a monster
But everyone was very afraid of him
Because everyone *knew* he was a monster
And not just any monster
A terrifying monster
He had many fangs in his mouth
And only one normal tooth
He had many friends including humans
Animals and more animals
But he liked the humans
Because they gave him more food
Than the animals.

Aqsa Ahmad (8)
Lathom Junior School

The Fleshlump Eater

On the dark side of Jupiter
Lives the Fleshlump Eater
It has five eyes and is naughty
It makes you feel rather peculiar

It is a shape-shifter
That turns into any shape you want
Cat, dog or rabbit
It will be nice and give you a munch
And you will grab it - like a rabbit
If you are nice it'll give you a crunch
From its gooey, out-of-date carrot

Go to Jupiter and you will find
A monster with goo on its head
Try not to think of it
Being under your bed.

Ashia Hassan Dhinbil aden (7)
Lathom Junior School

Super-Duper Friendly Monsters

All people think that
Monsters are scary and mean
But you should give them a chance
To show you who they are
All monsters need is a
Chance, chance, chance.
So next time you see one
Give them a high five
Fluffy Foxy lives in the coolest place ever
Disneyland
Over there she meets
New and exciting people
They sing, they dance, they waddle
They play for a whole new day
So there you have a
Friend, friend, friend.

Zara Waqar Bhatti (8)
Lathom Junior School

The Mysterious Monster

My Mysteeker came from far away
She came looking for someone to play
She glowed so bright
In the darkness of the night
She was an awesome sight
I went towards her with a racing heart
Her eyes were loving from the start
She saw I was in fear
And in her eyes I saw a tear
I knew then she wouldn't hurt me
I knew then a good friend she would be
I held her hand which was so furry
Off we went to play in a hurry.

Amaara Sana Jabar (7)
Lathom Junior School

The Slimy Monster

She was stinky
Her eyes were bendy
The monster was gooey and slimy
Stella's breath smelled
As slimy as a dribble dragon
She was nasty and roared like a dragon
Pointy antennae, sharp
They all lived near Bloop
There was a nice monster there too.

Maheen Saqib (8)
Lathom Junior School

The Dream That Became A Nightmare

The hairy monster called Hideous Hydra,
Comes from Planet Hogruezome.
His grotesque appearance quivers the world,
Stopping happiness from reaching us.
His movements are as fast as lightning,
Roars as deafening as thunder.
Whenever he stares at you,
Fire is sure to shoot.
His rotten fingernails snarl menacingly,
His razor-sharp teeth grit threateningly.
He has a dream to eliminate the human race,
To rule our fabulous world.
He has millions of blood-curdling henchmen
By his side, ready to face battle.
Our fearless leader approaches to settle
This for once and all.
Bloodstains cover the battlefield,
Men lie desperately on the ground.

The monster uses his stare of fire,
We fight back with our shields of justice.
Our leader surreptitiously sneaks
Behind the monster,
Stabbing him to the ground.
The devilish monster coughs up blood,
Killing himself instantly.
We celebrate over our victory
Upon this special day,
Forever and ever and ever.

Dillani Arulananthan (10)
Marvels Lane Primary School

Helping Hand

I'm from Natlpeed, I live near an outdoor zoo
I have lots of friends, but they don't look like me
Because I'm extraordinary.
I have special powers, sometimes that's cool
But other times it's not the best.
I'm yellow in colour and only have one eye
A snout for my nose that helps me find my way
I have a desire to help
And my nose helps me sniff it out
When someone's in trouble I'm there no doubt
As quick as a flash I can help anyone out.
My teeth are sharp but not to hurt
Helping others is the trade of my game
And also I haven't told you my name.
"Nice to meet you, I'm glad you came
I will share with you my name, I am Zayne!
My favourite food is honey and grain
This gives me more superpowers
That enter my brain.
I drink lots of water to keep hydrated

I have the longest tongue you have ever seen
If you're in trouble, you can count on me.

Eris Gyan (11)
Marvels Lane Primary School

Monster, Monster, Where Are You?

Monster, monster, where are you?
With your pretty eyes, ever so blue
Fluffy fur, head to toe
Where you are, only you know.

Be my friend and let us play
Please before the break of day
You are a unique creature
With your vibrant colours
That is your greatest feature.

You are great in every way
I beg you to please stay
We will do many things as a team
You are like a creature from a dream.

You are smart and adored by your peers
I promise you that together, you'll never be in tears
We will be great friends, that I assure
Together we can do the impossible and more.

You are really lovely and creative
And if you change I will still be supportive
Be my friend and let us play
I beg you to come and stay, May.

Chelsea Amankwah (11)
Marvels Lane Primary School

The Cutest Monster

Monster, monster, are you there?
OMG, you're really here!
You're on the bed
You're on my head...
Go away and don't come back...
Actually, you're kinda cute
I'll keep you and call you Jack.

To others you're hairy and scary
But to me you're as harmless as a fairy
Your fur is soft, long and curly
And although you're a boy, you seem girly.

Shall we be friends?
You can share my room with me
And when you're hungry
You can even share my tea.

Monster, monster, you're really here
And we'll still be best friends
This time next year
You're cute, you're fuzzy, you're pink and blue
I'll never find a better friend than you.

Teigan Stuart (11)
Marvels Lane Primary School

The Fiend Of Flames

Through its head poked out a tusk,
But the dragon only came out at dusk,
Upon people, the beast had climbed,
And ate everyone it could find.
All the women, kids and men,
Never to be seen again,
It wielded a mighty, long tail,
As long as the longest veil.
"The fang-like snakes they are,
Yet the creature doesn't lurk far!"
That's when the public started to stand back!
That's when the public started to attack!
That's when the public started to revolt!
All mighty, like a lightning bolt!
The threat was then killed,
Taken and grilled.
That night the beast,
Was turned into a giant feast.

Rupertas Brazdzius (11)
Marvels Lane Primary School

My One And Only Magical Friend... Shimmer!

Your eyes are as elegant as feathers,
Your smiles are as sparkly as diamonds.
Your fur is smooth like silk,
Your horn is as strong as love.

Oh Shimmer, you're my only friend,
As sweet as chocolate, as soft as velvet,
Oh Shimmer, you're my precious gem,
As beautiful as an angel.

How your footwork glides
Across the sugary sherbet,
Twirling in the sweetened air.
How your milk-white wings shine
Through the glossy river streams,
The queen of dancing stars.

Your eyes are as elegant as feathers,
Your smiles are as sparkly as diamonds.
Your fur is as smooth as silk,

For you are my one and only magical friend...
Shimmer!

Jathursa Satkunarasa (11)
Marvels Lane Primary School

Double Trouble

Double Trouble and Gobble Hobble
Sometimes hate each other
But always are double, together and forever.
Double Trouble was born in the town
'Stranger Things'
I'm glad he hasn't eaten any rings.
Gobble Hobble will sometimes help
But not always when he is having a yelp.
If you saw him, you would scream
But make sure you don't start to steam.
He loves his family to death
Makes a promise
And doesn't stop to take a breath.

Ariana Ioana Popovici (11)
Marvels Lane Primary School

The Lonely Monster

He was a really, really lonely monster,
'Cause his horns were part of a lobster.
He looked like a fly,
So everyone said goodbye,
As he was from a different world,
Where he was a slave,
In the underworld.

He scared the kids,
By eating the pigs.
As the kids sat,
He took them as breakfast,
But after a change of mind,
He let them free.

After that day,
He sat with humans in May.

Salvijus Brazdzius (9)
Marvels Lane Primary School

The Creature

Over the altitudes of the hill,
Comes a creature,
With eyes as charming as puppies,
Razor-sharp fangs from unimaginable beasts,
Scabrous skin as dark as genuine evil,
Enchanted wings from entrancing fairies,
Muscular legs holding the creature,
Up to its full height,
The features can only belong to one such thing,
Sid!

Jennifer Wang (10)
Marvels Lane Primary School

The Greek Monster From Hell

H er eyes were a gift from Satan, burning red,
E very moment with her made the world fill with dread.
L osing your mind was a normal thing,
P eople quivered at the sight of her venomous sting.

M onsters nearby who ran soon became assassinated,
E very mortal didn't stand a chance, they were annihilated.

Farhiya Hassan (10)
Mitchell Brook Primary School

Smelly Bob

Big, bright Bob likes green,
Sometimes he is mean,
But he is mostly unclean.

Bob is hairy and smelly
But also sometimes friendly.
Don't be scared of his horns,
They're only spiky like thorns.

When we play I like to run away.
He runs and runs into a lunge
To try and get me.

Carina Carter (6)
Mitchell Brook Primary School

The Poffaglemoffloft

P lease come and see him
O n school days, he meets his friend, Tim
F un things are always there
F licking off dewdrops, one of his leaves tears
A gony fills his body with *no ideas*
G rowling, the teacher says, "Use Wikipedia!"
L ovely mist fills him with joy
E cstatic children get him a toy
M ilk chocolate, to him tastes so delicious
O n the car ride home, he feels malicious
F unny and nice in all the ways
F ierce and protective of all his friends
L oss of words
O n the trip to the farm, he sees a lot of nerds
F inal days, all so fun
T rees grow, all because of his sun.

Namitha Lakshmikantham Arava (9)
Notre Dame Catholic Primary School

Marvellous Disco-Oozy

Oh Disco-oozy, your skin is slimy like goop,
And your jelly eyes go round in a loop.
Your curly hair is as fluffy as fur,
And your silver cat always purrs.

Your body shines like a star in the sky,
You make wishes come true whilst you fly.
Your bushy unibrow sticks on your head,
You turn off your brightness when you go to bed.

Your scaly feet tap on the floor,
The crowd keeps asking for more.
Your golden crown sits on his hair,
You've always dreamed of going to a funfair.

Valina John (9)
Notre Dame Catholic Primary School

Mayhem Maya

Mayhem Maya, she's around
Always doing mayhem, such a clown
Yelling at the people away from town
Hopping and stopping the buildings going down
Echoing everywhere the people shout
Mayhem Maya is about
Lock your doors and blow candles out.

Maya is left alone crying and moaning
All the people open up
But only a tiny boy has feelings
So you know, you can come on
And help this mythical creature out
All the people come and play
With Mayhem Maya all day.

Chara Ibeauuchi (9)
Notre Dame Catholic Primary School

Dino Dan On The Hunt

Dino Dan on the hunt,
Dino Dan doing a stunt,
Crash, crash, the wind blew,
Crash, crash, the wind flew.

There are silly monsters,
Chilly monsters,
You can't believe your eyes,
When they do their stunts.

I can't believe this is happening,
Although the monsters are tapping,
Dino Dan on the hunt,
Dino Dan, doing the stunt.

Jedi Olaose (9)
Notre Dame Catholic Primary School

The Cheap Monster

The monster who had bulging eyes
Got a very big surprise
She went upstairs to see what was wrong
Her mum was dancing all night long
The monster who was white and pink
She went downstairs and *blink, blink, blink*
The little monster called the cheesy police
They brought a lot of squawky geese
They took her mum in a filthy car
Then they put her behind steel bars
Mum's eyes were pouring with salty tears
Oh she had some very big ears
What a cheeky little girl
Now Mum was gone so she could swirl
She went upstairs to get her dress
And she made an awful mess
Now the monster wanted to dance
In the room downstairs she was ready to prance.

Edith Christie (9)
Rosemary Works School

Gooey Green

Gooey Green is from Mashville
And he is very bashful,
He likes to swim, climb and swing
And his favourite food is the Haribo ring.

Gooey Green is very lean,
He has the longest arms I've ever seen.
All of his hair grows straight up in the air,
He can shape-shift to look like a mare.

So Gooey Green went to town
To buy himself a fancy ballgown
For he was going to the Queen's best ball.
It would be lovely, he'd love it all.
But when he got there, everyone stared,
And that's when Gooey Green started to glean
That everyone there was being so mean
Just because his dress was not green.

Poor Gooey Green and his pink dress
They ripped it up into tiny shreds.
"Oh no, oh no, I think I'm dead,
I'll get them for this and they will dread."

He cried in the corner for a day and a night
Until he awoke with a great big sigh.
"I'll go now!" he said. "I know the time is right."
So he jumped on his feet and walked through the night.

Eleanor Stewart
Rosemary Works School

Gonnog

Capable of flight
He has colossal might
The day he was born
Was tragic and forlorn
He can turn into a goat
And sing a minor note
He mated with a giant tick
Whose brother was nicknamed 'Cool Nick'
His kid is now named Jeff
Jeff likes the treble clef
Jeff looks like a wreck
His friend is a human named Deck
Gonnog is a treasure trove
Of stories from around the globe
He lives in a haunted ravine
That is so amazingly green
He looks so funny in his hut
His dog is such a lovely mutt
When you see him be warned that
He really loves his tacky hat.

Sam Maguire (9)
Rosemary Works School

Devi

Horns of the devil
Teeth as sharp as a buzz saw
A heart bought from eBay

Highly lazy, only likes
Couch potatoes, especially
Video gamers

Pugnacious and rude
Cruel, mean and loquacious
Enough of that, it's painful.

Oliver Altan Bulus (9)
Rosemary Works School

My Coughing Monster

Torture was as red as a cherry,
and was very, very merry.
His fire was as hot as a big boiling pot.
Little Torture and his friends,
went to the place where the valley ends.
Into the forest they went, where they smelt a scent.
It was the flowers held by Mr Beaver,
and poor little Torture had hay fever!
He sneezed and coughed and coughed and sneezed,
till he fell to his small, scaled knees.
Fire scared his friends Scorture and Buddy,
and they ran away, getting very muddy.
I found poor Torture all alone,
and took him home in spite of his moans.
I gave him coffee, I gave him tea,
I even gave him some honey.
But he cried and clenched his tummy,
Hmm... I knew what he wanted: Mummy!

I looked in the forest and guess what I found?
Torture's mummy, safe and sound!
Torture went to wake his mum,
Climbing on her big red tum.
Oh, my coughing monster! I thought,
But I ought to go, I really ought!
Torture cuddled up to his mum,
On top of her cherry tum.

Maja Agnieszka Lockwood (10)
St Bernadette RC Junior School

The BFFM

A monster haunts you in the night
And in your dreams
But every monster is not what it seems
Once a BFFM came to my dream
It was the best experience I ever had
The BFFM was actually a monster
But friendly indeed
The name was Crummy
It rhymed with tummy
He was generous and blue
And purple too
He was my new best friend
He was forced to be mean by his parents
But I told him, "You can be who you want to,
Just follow your dream."
We became best friends
In an everlasting end
He was really kind and also fluffy
Just like my teddy
We went on many adventures because
He was brave, he was my best friend

That I ever had, until Crummy had to go home
I named Crummy the BFFM
(Big Fluffy Friendly Monster)
He was such a good friend
That's why I'll never forget
The adventures we had together.

Tia Scott-Lewis (10)
St Bernadette RC Junior School

Where's Shelly?

Where's Shelly, is she in my belly?
If she is, then she's very smelly.
Shelly is a shape-shifter and her friend is a weight-lifter.
Shelly always gets in trouble
Because Shelly's a little devil.
She's very bossy
And her friend's name is Mossy!
Is she with Mossy
Or is she just being bossy?
She's bad
And she gets very mad.
But where's Shelly?
I feel sick to my belly.
People think Shelly is smelly
But she thinks people have really fat bellies.
Ring a bell
Then you'll know that Shelly's in a well.
Shelly likes to doodle
And she has a pet poodle.

Is she behind the bush?
Because it looks like a big blob of mush.
Shelly's friends are looking for her everywhere
But hopefully we'll find a penny there!
I found Shelly
She was stuffing her belly!
Naughty Shelly!

Yesheemah Constantine
St Bernadette RC Junior School

The Monster Called Gothan

There was a monster called Grothan
That lived in a dark, damp cave
The monster was alone and scared
For he travelled far and wide
To have someone to share with for once

One day the monster went further
He went back to his home and knew
He was alone forever
He knew he was scared of being alone
He knew he was scared of having no one
He knew he wanted someone

For he was fluffy and smelt like candyfloss
But he didn't understand
Why people didn't like him
He knew he was fluffy, huge, generous, cute
And intelligent to other people
He knew people never knew
He was a kind one inside

In the end he found someone new
They played and did everything together

They knew that each other had no one
But they were happy to have
Someone beside them and to have
Someone to be there for them.

Jahzae Barnes (9)
St Bernadette RC Junior School

My Invisible Dragon

I have an invisible dragon
She's such a remarkable flyer
She soars through the sky
On invisible wings
Exhaling invisible fire
My dragon is utterly silent
She soundlessly swoops through the air
Why, she could be flying beside you right now
And you'd never know she was there
And if you should reach out to pet her
I don't think she'd notice you too much
Her body is simply too hairy
And light to sense her by movement or touch
And just if you don't see her
And just as she cannot be felt
My dragon does not have an odour at all
Which means she will never smell
Although you may find this outlandish
You just have to trust me, it's true
And oh, by the way, did I mention
I have an invisible unicorn too?

Anastasia Peters Macauley (7)
St Bernadette RC Junior School

Benji The Lonely Beast

Benji is a kind monster
Of course, you'll think he's an imposter
But to be honest, he just tries his best
To be like all the rest.

All his life, he's been pushed away
Even though he just wants to play!
Happy and joyful on the outside
But cold and lonely on the inside.

"Go away!"
That's all he's been told...
Finally, Benji starts to think it through
What to think, what to do.

So finally, Benji decides not to hold on, but to let go
For there is nothing he can do but sit in his cave
With his family and his two friends
Poor old Benji, what is he to do?

Samantha Motato (10)
St Bernadette RC Junior School

Spiky

There is a monster named Spiky
He smells like Skittles
He is a shape-shifter
Who has the brain of a human
He can teleport
I saw him once
He was in a candy shop
He made me smell him
When he shape-shifted
Into a human
Then he took me!
He had normal teeth
I was gone for a week
So no one heard a peep
But when I got home
I told everyone
But they wouldn't believe
When he gets angry
He goes black and red
But his normal colours
Are blue and white

His spikes pop up
And his teeth are white
We calmed him down
We put him on a cloud
He fell asleep
So we didn't make a peep
Before we left the sky
We said, "Goodnight."

Tahirah Heron (10)
St Bernadette RC Junior School

Jimmy

Jimmy lives in a cave
That is very dark
He is very grumpy and lonely
With very sharp teeth
He is evil and doesn't like people
They make him angry.

He changes colour
When people make him angry.
He is wicked
The worst part is that
He has spikes, and when people
Make him angry
His spikes come out really long.

He smells like rubbish in a trash can.
When you touch him, his fur is really soft
And he is really hairy.

Don't talk to him because
He is very evil and grumpy.
If, someday, you see him with your friends

Just don't say anything
Just run away from him.

Isabella Quintero (9)
St Bernadette RC Junior School

The Graveyard Raven

I know a monster who's mad
He stalks anyone in his territory
Who's psycho and bad
And sends you to purgatory.
He's a raven, human-sized
Who'll take you for a ride
He stalks graveyards at night
He really hates light.
So as a child goes in
His life goes out
Because he devours his skin
Making murder most foul.
His glowing, purple eyes
See people beyond the grave
A nice lunch and dinner
He wishes to crave
So be careful when wandering
The graveyard, rich or poor
Or else four words
Will haunt your mind like a roar
Says the raven, nevermore.

Jotham Osorio (9)
St Bernadette RC Junior School

Haunted John

One day in a deep, damp cave
Lived a monster and its name was John
It loved to haunt people every day and night
People said that it turned invisible and enormous
John loved to be terrifying and spooky.

John was brave but grumpy
He was not friends with other monsters
He was unfriendly every day
His fur was fluffy like a cloud.

I walked closer and closer to the cave
At one glance there was a monster
I looked again and it was gone
I wondered where it went
It never appeared when I left
It was never to be found
Until the next day, I was being haunted.

Evelyn Romo Vosas (10)
St Bernadette RC Junior School

The Angel Demon...

I spot a monster here,
I spot a monster there,
But there's something white and fluffy in the distance...
It looks like a cute little fuzzy angel!
Oh wait... why did it throw a bucket of water on top of that monster?
It acts completely like a...
Devil!
Argh! Run away!
It's trying to put goo on me!
Why did I decided to come to this... devilish place?
Um, I just realised it's called D... D...
Demonville!
It has loads of mischievous demons!
That monster looks like an angel,
But it acts like a demon,
I shall call it...
The Angel Demon!

Melissa Ocampo (10)
St Bernadette RC Junior School

Jeremy The Monster

Jeremy the monster was ferocious and wild
He loved chaos and drama
Jeremy smelt like rotten eggs
Which stank everywhere he went.

He was hairy and green
Just like slimy cream
Jeremy's claws were as sharp as knives
And he was as angry as a gorilla.

Jeremy was ugly and spiky
He could camouflage into the bushes
And he was eight feet tall
A cold-hearted monster that thought he was cool.

He came from Planet Bong
Their favourite instrument was a gong!
Jeremy was as lonely as a cloud
That said, "Hi," out loud.

Yamrot Legesse Daniel (10)
St Bernadette RC Junior School

Monster

I was in my bedroom, staring into space,
and then I tied my shoelace.
When I was doing it, I heard a sound,
so I looked round and round.

Next I felt something weird,
something like a hairy beard.
Then I saw a hairy boy,
who had an awesome toy.

After I saw the true vision,
that didn't involve my tuition.
Next I saw a hairy monster, so big and fat.
You don't know what happened after that.

I looked up and saw,
a cute monster who looked like a boar.
After we became friends,
looks like there was a happy end.

Antwarn Philippe-Watson (10)
St Bernadette RC Junior School

Fluff Fangs

Deep down in Torture Town lives Fluffy Fangs,
Torture Town is as dark as night, even in the day,
There live other monsters, very scary,
Fluffy Fang's dad is called Lary,
Fluffy Fangs is fluffy and pink,
And in the night, she likes to play tricks,
With her best friend Gudaliwin and brother Micks.
Her fangs nearly cover half her head,
She likes to play tricks on humans all night long,
But is very friendly most of the day,
And her birthday is in May.
When she plays tricks, her parents make her pay,
But that is just Fluffy Fangs' way.

Ciara Murphy (10)
St Bernadette RC Junior School

Lexi

Lexi was born in a bush
As bushy as hair
His fluffy skin was red
And he shared his brother's bed
His teeth were as yellow
As the sun
He tricked his parents
And had a little fun
When he was in school
He was as rude as a bear
And when it came to tests
He thought it wasn't fair
When he was a teenager
He entered a band
And when he was mistaken
His brother gave him a hand
He grew up some more
And became a man
Then he thought to buy a van
He found himself his own lady
And then he got a baby!

Noel Chiagozie Opurum (8)
St Bernadette RC Junior School

The Twisted

Long ago in Dusty Divot,
A creature got killed by a man,
He turned it robotic,
A killing machine,
It is now a guard,
Of an evil master,
It can kill, it's smart,
No one can escape,
Anyone who enters its area,
Will never leave,
You can try, but you can't hide,
It'll always seek, always find,
No one is strong enough to beat it,
Not even its master,
Can take it down,
Run, run, run as fast as you can,
But you'll die,
Even if you try,
It's time to die now, bye.

Oliwier Szczekala (10)
St Bernadette RC Junior School

Spiky

I have a friend, his name is Spiky
He is very clever, he is very shiny
He lives under my bed in a magic forest
He likes flowers and eats porridge
He is a good monster
He runs and is a boxer
He protects us
From scary stuff
He can roll into a ball
With double spikes and horns
He goes to school
In the afternoon
He enjoys being first
He is the best
I have a friend with a big heart
He is very friendly and very smart
He loves us, he is a big one
We play a lot, we have fun.

Samuel Martin Muñoz (8)
St Bernadette RC Junior School

Fluffy The Great And Puffy

Once there was a monster called Fluffy
He lived in Monsterville where everyone was puffy
He was orange and he liked to eat porridge
He could transform into a fluff ball so
His friends could play 'puff a ball'
When it was dark he grew and the dogs barked
His friend Nuff, she was always puffing off
Her dad said, "Tough, I've had enough."
Monsterville was one of the three monster towns
We didn't pay pounds, we paid monster towns
Fluffy was invisible but I called him visible.

Megan Murphy (8)
St Bernadette RC Junior School

The Toxic Slayer Poem

Once, I sat in my house thinking,
Where should I attack next?
And then I said, "Why don't I attack Superman's base?"
So off I set to his base,
Like a sneaky mouse looking for some cheese.

Then I finally arrived,
With nothing else to think of,
Only to kill,
There I saw him on his computer, checking something,
Then in I came and then, *shhum!*
He was dead.

He was lying on the floor,
And then I said,
"Who can stop me now?"

Kevin Gryniewicz (10)
St Bernadette RC Junior School

Monster Vano

In the deep dark lies a monster
He has lots of fur and is strong
His name is Vano the monster
He feels brave and cool, but he is most of all small.

I've seen him, he is very frightening
He only comes when you're asleep
No one has ever seen him
Except for me.

He crawls in the room
In the closet, in the bed
He might be there
But one day, he will be caught.

He lies under the bed
With covers that are red
And he will creep up
To be fed.

Max Fernandes (10)
St Bernadette RC Junior School

Uncontrollable Feti The Stealer

The evil creature was like a thief
It had dirty, sharp and decayed teeth
Its eyes were lava-red
It was hungry and needed to be fed
So, as quiet as a mouse, he went to his tent
People didn't like him because he was ugly
He cried with sadness, he just wanted a buddy
One day, I saw him crying and sighing
I went to him, "Why are you crying?"
Feti said, "I want a friend, I'm trying!"
I promised that I would be his friend,
Forever and ever until the end.

Paula Anais Campoverde (8)
St Bernadette RC Junior School

Be Aware!

The gruesome Undertaker was walking
Then he heard a girl talking
He asked the girl for help
But she yelped and yelped and yelped
Then he heard an astonishing sound
Was magic on this very ground?
It was the girl that had powers
That could set him free from the tower
The girl was delicate like a flower
The royal guards ran and came
They knew who to blame
Be aware
He will give you a scare
Keep your eyes open
You never know when your heart will be broken.

Admire Goswell (9)
St Bernadette RC Junior School

Dare Devil's Dares

The Dare Devil loves to dare
So everyone, beware!
He gets his name from his devilish eyes
But he hates the buzzing of flies.
His breath is dangerous, almost like it's poisonous
His skin is as black as charcoal and his mouth is like a dark hole
Just a little sniff and you are dead
His toxic breath he'll spread.
Valentine is more like a best friend
Because this monster has a big head.
If he sees you
And you try to flee
Your flesh is what he'll eat.

Whitney Amankwah Youles (9)
St Bernadette RC Junior School

The Dangerous Dragon

Once, in a cave as creepy as the end of the world,
A dragon lived there,
She had guns at her back and shooting black breath,
That was venomous and could kill you if you smelt it.
She lived in the Shadow Dragon Forest,
And she had three friends as ugly as bins,
They'd bully together,
Her friends were called Malia, Kayla and Amanda.
Dangerwar Dragon was the most wanted dragon,
For killing humans,
She was a danger to the humans,
And she was a killer.

Paula Andrea Segura (10)
St Bernadette RC Junior School

The Lonely Monster

One day a monster entered a cave
I was feeling very brave
So I went in
But inside it looked like a bin

This monster had gigantic teeth
But it was allergic to beef
I did not know what to think
Other than its mouth was as big as a sink

I hoped this monster had a brain
Or it would experience a lot of pain
The monster must have asked in shame
If I wanted to play a game
He was alone for the rest of his life
And never found a wife.

Caleb Michael Asare (10)
St Bernadette RC Junior School

Devil Darlin'

Now, sticks and stones may break your bones,
but behind the hedge lives a monster town,
the scariest of them all may make you frown,
but it's not a bad dream, he's a killer clown!
Of course, one of them might be funny,
and they're bigger than an overgrown bunny.
He's got a round green eyeball on his tongue,
he'll scare you so bad you'll lose a lung!
He's freaky, he's wacky, he's always there,
so you must always beware.

Daniel Forson Fosu (10)
St Bernadette RC Junior School

Buster, My Boy

Buster my boy
He looks like a toy
He's very fluffy
I call him Buffy
He's very smart
We can never be apart
He likes to laugh and prance
And also dance
He twists
He spins
He turns around
He gets dizzy and
Falls on the ground
If he sees bees
In the flowers
He gets magic powers
He kills it, he wins it, yes it all
Buster my boy, he looks like a toy
My best friend
Buster my boy.

Isabella Pereira (9)
St Bernadette RC Junior School

The Mysterious Monster

The monster wandered lonely as a cloud
As lonely as he could ever be
Then he saw a crowd
He could see

Dabe was as kind as a bunny
He was as hairy as a bear
He flew like a bird
And was as soft as a pillow

But everybody said he was so lovely
But he was always
Cosy and happy
Like me all the time

He was left in a damp, back cage
No one liked him
But inside he was very kind.

Beatriz Ferreira (10)
St Bernadette RC Junior School

The Merciful Monster

J'aaliyah wandered lonely as a cloud
As lonely as she could ever be
But then she saw a crowd
She could see

She was as friendly as a flower
But on the inside she was sour
So she climbed up a tower
To get more power

Her claws were as sharp as knives
But she was as short as an ant
So she could climb into people's pants
But she would always be remembered
As The Merciful Monster.

Dionne Boateng (10)
St Bernadette RC Junior School

The Glumsly, The Cute Monster

An ugly monster lived in the forest
He was called Glumsly
He was smelly and ate dog food
Although he was a friendly creature
All the children were terribly scared of him
Once the monster appeared under my bed
He was smelly but friendly
It was bedtime, so my mummy came
And said, "Goodnight."
All the children were afraid
But not me
As Glumsly and I were
Best mates.

Maria Iwan (10)
St Bernadette RC Junior School

The BFG

Once in the woods I saw
This monster but it was an imposter.
He was lonely as a fly
Always looking for pie
As friendly as a pussycat
Who only wanted a friend.

The only thing he wanted
Was someone that could understand him
He met a girl named Daisy
And soon they were to wed
Friendship, love, togetherness grew
And the BFG was welcomed by all.

Alexandru Andrei Cirstea (9)
St Bernadette RC Junior School

The Sick Ghost

I know a ghost who stays in bed all day,
He's always tired and doesn't want to play,
His name is Philip and this is the reason why,
Philip won't move out of bed, even if we tried.
He is always sick,
As the clock goes *tick-tick*.
So this is the story,
But have I told you about Dory?

Leticia Gouveia (10)
St Bernadette RC Junior School

Nazgûl

Deep in the land of Mordor,
What lies?
For Sauron's gaze,
Petrifies.
The Nazgûl roam Mordor,
Where they go,
All land dies,
The eagles flee,
So will you and I.
The Nazgûl roam,
Once, nine kings there were,
But Sauron betrayed them,
As he betrayed me.

Luke Adams (9)
St Bernadette RC Junior School

The BDJ

The BDJ lived in a dark, smelly, cold cave
He was exploring in the hoods of the woods
At a glance I saw the monster
We became friends for life
I was not afraid and nor was he
And we became husband and wife

I told him never be afraid
Never be afraid of people
Animals or ghosts.

Asiâ-Léigh Hayles-Chin (9)
St Bernadette RC Junior School

The Invisible Monster

There was a monster who was wild and black
His name was Sam
He wasn't an ordinary monster
He could cut through wood and trees
And be invisible
So don't be afraid
If he comes to your door
But if you are frightened
Then he will take you away.

Dainah Georgia Dyer (10)
St Bernadette RC Junior School

Cheeky

Cheeky was like a mouse
That could never be caught
Wherever he was
He was always the cheekiest
He had mischievous thoughts
Of all, he was the furriest
Because being unfriendly many times
He thought he still wanted to be the cuddliest.

Rufta Angosom (9)
St Bernadette RC Junior School

My Monster

My monster is big
My monster wears a wig
My monster is blue
And it has a big shoe.
My monster is cute
And she plays the flute.
My monster is scary
And my monster's
Called Mary!

Ruby Hanson (8)
St Bernadette RC Junior School

The Book Bag Creeper

Inside your book bag he hides,
Waiting and lurking inside,
Mysterious and squeaky,
He's very, very sneaky,
Inside your book bag he hides.

Two heads, both small in size,
Both ready to tell great lies,
One for smell, the other for sight,
Giving you an unsuspecting fright,
Inside your book bag he hides.

Add in your stationery just over an ounce,
I sure can tell you he'll be ready to pounce,
From felt tips to colouring pens,
Once he eats it, they'll all end,
Even your pencil case will soon be erased,
Inside your book bag he hides.

Keno Agbandje (11)
St Chad's RC Primary School

Invisible Zogdog

"A new monster is born!"
cried the nurse,
But it was born with a
terrible curse.
Its belly was filled
with grotesque colours,
It had to be hidden rapidly
from others.
Studiously, the nurse headed
with the ugly baby south,
Her wit was as quick
as a greyhound's mouth,
Where all the peculiar people went,
The baby monster was sent.
She was off to the
Institute of Madness,
Knowing she was awkward
filled her with sadness,
They became invisible
straightaway,

And no one will ever
forget the day,
When they named her
'Invisible Zogdog',
No one would see her
emerge from the fog.

In the capital, munching, manic
she carried on her life,
Someone almost sliced her
with a knife!
One special day, the system
broke down,
This left her with
a frown.

Now her secret was
revealed,
When people passed by
they squealed,
A little monster
raising her head,

She shakily said,
"I really love you
for who you are.
Do you want to get a drink
at the Monster Bar?"
Invisible Zogdog knew
she had found a friend,
Who would be there
'til the end.

Theresa-Mae Brown
St Chad's RC Primary School

Friendly Scares

Little Scares was born
on Planet Zog
filled with monsters
and tricky fog.
Every night, he would wish upon a star
to go down to Earth
and come back with no scar.
Little Scares was worried how
he would be treated
if he would be hurt
or if he would be cheated.
So he went down to Earth
excited about what he would find
thinking very cautiously
oh, what a curious mind!
First time the humans saw him
they said something not nice
chattering, "Oh, a monster
he might have lice!"

Michelle Appiah Arhin (8)
St Chad's RC Primary School

The Dream Girl Princess Demon Called Dream

In the darkness of the night,
shadows are appearing and disappearing.
When I whisper,
you shiver,
you think it's just a sound,
but you don't know I'm around.

The children fear,
then I reappear,
I say,
"Do not be afraid,
I am here to bring presents every day."
The children are filled with joy,
they are not scared of the monster called Dream any more.

I am truly a dream come true,
I am the princess of dreams too,
I am not scary,
or hairy,
my claws might be sharp,

but I am sweet with chubby cheeks,
I'll bring you presents forever,
and I'll not be scary ever.

Dream big,
and all the nightmares,
will come,
out of you.

Now the shadows on the walls,
are signs of your friend Dream,
coming towards you,
to give you presents,
and reward you.

Ayen Achiri-Ngu (8)
St Chad's RC Primary School

My Mouth

One mouth likes to chat
one mouth likes to giggle
one mouth likes to chew
one mouth likes to whistle
one mouth likes to beg
one mouth likes to lie
one mouth likes to gossip
one mouth is demanding fries
one mouth loves to eat sugar
one mouth likes to eat my boogers
one mouth likes to moan about my leg
one mouth loves to eat egg
one mouth likes to eat ice cream
one mouth wishes it shot laser beams
my mouths talk over each other
so sit down and stay
because they might take all day!

Jeffrey Osei-Owusu (9)
St Chad's RC Primary School

Harmain

Monsters can be scary and have sharp teeth
but not this one, he is sweet.

His name is Harmain and he's very cute
even though he has three eyes
he winks with two.

Harmain is mischievous
but cares when you need it.
He's tough on the outside
but a big softy on the in.

My monster is blue and loves to give clues
Harmain is a great yeti and is very short.
Should he eat you, or shouldn't he...?
Won't that be a debate!

Adrianna Grace Pope
St Chad's RC Primary School

The News Of Something

A monster was born in mid-air
with eyes as bright as fire
and a body as light as a feather
but as strong as a diamond.
It walked as quiet as it could be
and approached a village.
Suddenly, it disappeared.
As it ran closer and closer
it reached its destination.
It did what it had to do
and began running, carrying
a person.
It was on the news
but more and more people
disappeared.
Until it was ready to eat.
Yum!

Ethan Czarnecki
St Chad's RC Primary School

Spike The Horrible Bear

Once, there was a bear named Spike
And he always spoilt people's shoes
He had grizzly fur which was blue
Spike had special amber eyes
And loved to nibble dirty flies!
His hair grew from flowerpots
And he loved to sleep a lot.
Spike had mouldy and rotten teeth
And for dinner, he liked to eat piles of meat.
Off he went into his dark and creepy cave
Whenever he'd lie down, his tummy looked like a wave.

Mercedes Ohenewah Abiana Agyiri (8)
St Chad's RC Primary School

My Best Friend And Me

Out of the white fluffy clouds came a smile, then an eye
and then a cute blue monster called Cuddles!
He was tiny and smart
you could pop him in a cart.
In his eyes, there was a hint of mischief.
He would peek out of the candyfloss
like puffs of gas
and giggle.
He sprang and leapt from cloud to cloud
screaming and shouting ever so loud.
He jumped up and down
so much he ought to have won a crown
for acting like a kangaroo.
He hopped down onto Earth
every morning and every night.
He snuck into the house
then up to my room
and I cuddled with him like a cushion
and slept with him every night.

But when my parents saw him
they got a fright!
Because a blue little monster
was at the end of my bed
with one of my hats on his head.
He is very funny
and very, very kind
ever since I saw him
we were in a bind.
That's why I love Cuddles
and he loves me.

Tia Simone Thomas (10)
St Mary's & St John's CE School

Fluffy The Lost Pet!

On the way to my house, I met
a wonderful, cute and fluffy pet.
She shouted and said
"I need to be fed!"
We rapidly ran to the shops
to buy her a big fat juicy chop.
She had no clothes, so I gave her a top
with a wonderful picture of a mop.
She had a light purple face
and had small shoes with a lace.
She loved tongue-twisters like
'Peter Parker picked a peck of pickled peppers.'
She said her favourite animals were woodpeckers
and she thought they were wreckers.
Then we decided to go to the park
to play on the lovely swings.
Then we were starving
so we bought some chicken wings.
Then it was getting dark
so we went home, but then we heard dogs bark.

The day came to an end
so I couldn't play with my friend.
Today was amazing
today was brill.
"Will you come back?"
She said, "I will."

Taneesha Ahmed
St Paul's Way Foundation School

A Day Out With A Rainbow Monster

On the way to school, I met
a lovely rainbow monster pet.
He was adorable and red
he also claimed he hadn't been fed
so we bought a delicious cake.
Suddenly
we realised it wasn't baked.
The next morning, Rainbow the likeable monster came to school
then he jumped into the cool, clear pool.
He asked my teacher to fly a kite
into the blue, bright sky.
In class, the jolly, energetic monster spoke
but the classroom was up in smoke.
The monster was cute
and he was neat.
Rainbow the sweet, polite monster was entertaining
but everyone was complaining.

We went to the calm park to play on the swings
after, we bought some chicken wings.
Today was just brill
I hope Rainbow visits again
he said he will.

Khalil Umar (8)
St Paul's Way Foundation School

Fireball

On my way to the bathroom, I met a rainbow French pet.
She said she accidentally came to London and was born in France.
The only thing she had was a photo of her parents.
I left her in my room and dressed her up and her name was Fireball.
She had a bet with my cat and won the bet and sat on my cat.
When I came back from the bathroom, Fireball gave me a weird stary stare.
She wasn't fed at all and was starving, fed up.
I gave her my pet cat's biscuits, but my cat got furious.
Sometimes, she was so funny that she would make my eyes all runny.
Every day, we would go on biscuity adventures.
Oh, Fireball, today was just amazing, today was just brill.
I hope we meet again, after all, she did say she would come every day.

Nishat Chowdhury (8)
St Paul's Way Foundation School

Me And My Pet

I went to a castle with my pet,
We went in and we were wet.

Me and my pet had breakfast,
My pet was in a blast!

My monster threw cuddly clothes everywhere,
The Queen came in and she had messy hair.

She was so angry, she roared with anger!
Her face was as red as a pair of red pliers!

The Queen turned into a nasty witch who was so prickly,
My monster became all tricky!

Then a superhero locked the Queen in a cage,
Then, after that, they were happy and they watched 'Rampage'.

My pet and me went downstairs,
Then we said, "Bye-bye, chairs!"

After that, we went back home,
To have a bath with lots of foam.

Ishrath Haque (8)
St Paul's Way Foundation School

Princess Popular's Day Out

On my way to the mall
I met a monster who had a ball.
I took her to the stall
and made an important call.
I asked where she got her make-up
and told her to shake up.
She started to be funny
and made my nose really runny.
She took me home
and used my phone.
She did my make-up
and made me shake up.
She showed her collection
and I showed my selection.
I looked in the mirror
and had lots of cheer.
We heard a knock on the door
and saw a spider on the floor.
After a long day
we said, "Hooray!"

Her name was Princess Popular
don't forget to say hey.
Today was amazing
today was just brill.
I hope she visits again
I mean, she said she will.

Ava Miah
St Paul's Way Foundation School

Annoying Monster

On my way home, I met,
A monster with six legs,
Five hands and two heads,
He was very spotty,
That made my brain go dotty,
When I put him in my bag,
He was jumping and bumping on the bag,
When I took my monster to school,
I used him because it was April Fool's,
Out of my bag he jumped,
And scared the teachers and students,
When we went back home,
The monster was getting violent.
Then he was silent,
When the monster was silent,
He started getting my phone.
After, we went to my room,
In the window, we saw a lady throwing a broom,
When it was evening, our mum said, "Goodnight!"
So I turned off my bedroom light.

Omer Ozturk (8)
St Paul's Way Foundation School

Mars FC

On the way to a football stadium,
I met a group, a monster football team,
The team captain's name was Firbly Gurgly.
They said they were from Mars,
So their team name was Mars FC.
They said they were going to play against my team,
And also, they said if they won,
They would take over the world.
I called my team over,
I told them about the monster football team,
They said, "We have to beat them."
So we had no choice but to save the world.
We got onto the pitch,
And started to play,
At the end of the day,
We managed to save the world,
So they left Earth and went to Mars.

Ahmad Ismailov (7)
St Paul's Way Foundation School

The Khaliliyed

On my way to the park,
I saw an ugly and terrible monster.
He was also friendly.
His name was Khaliliyed,
The monster said, "What's your name?"
I said, "My name is Mrs Myes."
I put him in bed,
But he had not been fed.
He asked for food,
And wore my shoes.
He liked tattoos,
And rotten poo,
And his mouth was covered in goo.
Also, he liked tongue-twisters,
Like 'Peter Piper picked a peck of pickled peppers.'
After a while, he had to go,
I said, "Will you come back?"
And he said, "Yes!"
I said, "Goodbye!"

Sulaiman Uddin (8)
St Paul's Way Foundation School

Goggler The Monster

On my way to school
I met a monster who
wore a hat
and petted a cat
and shouted
"What's your name?"
I answered
"Ahana!"
It looked like it wasn't fed
so I took it to the shops instead.
After we got a cake
we realised it wasn't baked!
We went to the park
and I realised Goggler had a mark.
Goggler bought chicken wings
then bought golden rings.
Today was just awesome
and today was so roarsome!
I hope Goggler visits again
I think I hear it shout, "I will!"

Ahana Zaina (8)
St Paul's Way Foundation School

Lovely

My monster was born on a sandy beach,
but she was very fluffy, soft and cuddly,
like a pillow, so she tried to get up,
but instead, a whoosh of wind blew her away,
and the whoosh of wind took her to a bus,
and she was making a fuss,
about it, but then she stopped fussing about the bus,
because the bus was going to a castle,
which was in Canada,
so she went in the castle,
but she couldn't make it through the whole way,
it took days,
the queen was a bit mean,
but she let the monster in the Canada castle.

Humayra Afsa (8)
St Paul's Way Foundation School

Queen Storm's Story With Me

On the way to cheerleading
I met a monster that was five foot six
she was bossy but lost.
She said she was American
and had an accent.
She said, "Feed me!
I eat flies."
So
we went to Asda to buy more flies
"Why eat flies when we have fly rice?"
"Can you be my friend?"
She said yes
and bought me a diamond
shiny friendship ring.
We went to the farm
to see cows
who tumbled down.
"Oh gosh! Gee whizz!"
We saw a flying pig.

Shyann Myrie (8)
St Paul's Way Foundation School

Firefluff's Lost Adventure!

On my way to the burning beach
I met a monster, tiny, yellow and peach
She said, "Help me, I'm lost!"
I replied, "I'll help you since you're tiny and lost."
She showed me to her home
She lived in a volcano.
The lava came alive
It took Firefluff back to her huge, hot home,
I waved goodbye,
Then her eyes glowed.
Today was awesome,
I hope Firefluff visits again,
She said, "It would be roarsome!"

Jannah Kolil Uddin (8)
St Paul's Way Foundation School

Adventure Time

On the way home, I met,
A new pet,
Who ended up on Earth,
On the day of his birth.

When the sun rose up,
He found his way out,
He saw the newspaper,
And wondered what was going to happen later.

He went to steal some jade jewels,
But unfortunately, he had a fall,
He said he wanted to go to Rome,
But then he said he wanted to go back home,
After he dropped his phone.

Ismail Hussain
St Paul's Way Foundation School

The Cool Dude

On the way home, I met,
a giant creature that was cool like a bull.
At that moment, the monster walked away,
he was in dismay.
Next, I brought my monster to school,
with some tools.
I hoped my friend wouldn't spill the beans,
and we hoped for lunch that it wasn't sardines!
In literacy, I had the shock of my life,
out came my monster with a fire knife!

Blake Power (7)
St Paul's Way Foundation School

Blue Panther

On the way to Marvel Studios
I met someone was was professional
at acting, he had a pet called Blue Panther.
When he was thirteen years old, he did a show
of him doing the floss from Fortnite
he wanted
to floss his teeth
to be clean.
When it was his birthday
his owner died
so Blue Panther was brave enough
to save someone
from the king alien.

Miraj Ishraq
St Paul's Way Foundation School

The Ink Day

On the way to school,
on the bus, a monster was fussy,
I met this monster,
with four arms, one eye, two legs,
he was going to the pool,
to swim and cool down,
then my monster went home,
with an ice cream cone and a bone,
Billy the bully bullied the monster,
with a monster toy called Chompster.

Daniel Fagbile (8)
St Paul's Way Foundation School

The Monster

It looks like a mangled, smashed sewer
Combined with a rotten jelly that has been rotten for millions of years!
If you ever meet him, you will be so mortified you will never be able to see daylight again!
He is so tall that his head is in space!
He eats all the planets.
It is dark because he eats the sun for dinner!
In the morning, the sun comes out of his mouth.
His teeth are as huge as a whale!
In space, it didn't use to be dark
The moon used to be as bright as a million suns
But his colossal hand squeezed the fire out, so now it is as dark as the ocean floor!
So if you meet him, you'll be sure you are not going to live!

Edoardo Walker (9)
The Dominie

The Monster Who Bites!

M is for money, it makes me rich
O is for obey, it makes me strict
N is for noise, it makes me shout
S is for sweet, it makes me lick
T is for terrified, it makes me roar
E is for enjoy, it makes me laugh
R is for rest, it makes me happy.

J is for jewels, which cover my eyes
E is for evil, it makes me cry
S is for scared, it makes me punch
S is for scent, it makes me scatter
I is for ill, it makes me spill
E is for easy, it makes me calm.

My name is Jessie and I hate playing games,
But be warned, I like to bite!

Amber Beauchamp (9)
The Dominie

The Flying Meaney

Whoever tries to shake his antenna will get electrocuted
He has wings and stinks of rotten eggs
He rides on a skateboard
Which has jet boosters on the back!
He looks cute and fluffy
But...

He is actually a Flying Meaney!
He has a giant spike
And has a thousand eyes
He has two million teeth
Which are as sharp as a spear!
He turns the floor into electricity
And shoots electricity from his antenna!
Argh!

Otto Matthias Ballard (7)
The Dominie

First Day At School

If was the first day of school
In the school called Cool School.
The monster packed his bag
With his baby bottle and his teddy monster
And he went to school in his buggy.
He saw the sign that said: *Cool School.*
He saw lots of other baby monsters
He saw a monster which was a fat cat with two heads!
Soon, it was home time
He told his mum he loved Cool School!

Sara Sonmez de Paz (7)
The Dominie

The Cookie Destroyer Of Fun

M is for mystery monster in the mountains
O is for odd, no ears or arms
N is for noisy when she shouts
S is for savage when she sees someone eating cookies
T is for teasing about the cookies being too good for children
E is for envious when she sees no cookies left
R is for rude when she snatches cookies from a child.

Nanna Marie Olsen (9)
The Dominie

Billey

B illey B is for big beast I saw
I stands for intelligence and impossible to beat
L stands for leader, he has never lost before
L stands for him not being lazy because he likes being evil
E stands for lots for enemies all over the Earth
Y stands for yelling so much when things go wrong, you can hear it from kilometres away!

Malachi Nunoo-Menash (9)
The Dominie

The Kindest Monster In Town

He might look mean, but he is the kindest monster in town.
He has a special tooth, the best tooth in town.
I met him once and thought how wonderful he was
And then he said, "Nice to meet you and see you around."
Two months later, he came back to town
And his special tooth fell out.
He gave it to me and we became
The best friends in town...

Monty Fisher (9)
The Dominie

Run

On one stormy night, I saw it.
It was whispering these words:
"Let me be what I want,
Let me be small,
Let me be tall.
When I say something twice,
Make me it..."
As fast as I could, I ran.
The monster fell in a hole,
And I caught it.
It got smaller,
I became what I destroyed.

Rafer Smith (8)
The Dominie

The Terror

T is for *terrifying*, I think to myself.
E is for eek! I shake in my body.
R is for razor-sharp teeth when he smiles.
R is for razor-sharp claws he scrapes on the wall.
O is for often he bites on his bones.
R is for the razor-sharp eyesight he has.

Taylor Caine-Hall (9)
The Dominie

The Flying Trickster

When someone touches him
They get zapped by his ticklish lasers!
His eyes are merry
And he is only six years old.
He asks to play with me in the playground
And I say, "Of course, let's go!"
We play on the swings
And fly a kite
He says that he will visit me again!

Rory Fitzsimons (7)
The Dominie

The Blob Of Death

The Blob is green and red
With an antler on his head
He is slimy like goo
And always says, "Boo!"
He bites you... but who?
He's tiny as a mouse
And lives in my house
His body is like broken glass
And he is the colour of grass
He is coming...
Argh!

Harry Deacon (8)
The Dominie

It's Coming!

M is for monster, it really is
O is for odd, a feeling I get
N is for naughtiness that it gets up to
S is for the sneaking it can do
T is for terrible, it might be
E is for egg, what it smells like
R is for ready, I am ready to run!

Alexander Hayes (7)
The Dominie

Spike

M - He is mysterious
O - Often, he has snow shooting out of his eye
N - For nasty
S - Snatch, give that back!
T - Trouble. Ah! Spike is coming!
E - Evil spike.
R - The rascal is coming to town! The rascal is coming to town!

Daniel Petrovic (9)
The Dominie

The Hibildy

As I was running to school
I saw a cute blob
With thirteen eyes
And one toenail
And out of that toenail came two antennae
That created a forcefield.
He was a disco monster!
If you were mean to him
He would
Do the 'Dance of Doom'!

Oscar Doernte (7)
The Dominie

Bobby

M is for monster that I saw
O is for, "Oh no, he's coming!"
N is for really nervous
S is for very scared
T is for really terrible
E is for very evil
R is for run fast!

Elina Eva Brown (9)
The Dominie

London's End

He is as blind as a bat
And as deaf as a post.
He destroys Central London
And he eats lots of toast!
He was born in 1919
And is *very* mean...
Argh!

Vincent Martini Fitzgerald (8)
The Dominie

The Sea Serpent Storm

A lonely ship sailing at sea,
Unaware of the dangers that were foretold.
Suddenly, a streak of lightning crosses the sky.
It starts to rain.
Out of nowhere, a horrendous shriek sounds from the watery depths.
Without warning, a thrashing, terrible force erupts from the glassy surface,
A sea serpent.
Lightning strikes, waves collide,
As the serpent pounds on the vessel.
Lives stand in the doors of death,
Some brave souls already vanquished and gone.
As the storm lashes out a whirlpool of death,
An ominous foreboding is felt at every breath.
As the horrifying creature advances,
Waves swim over the boat, drowning it,
So it can't even float.
As the serpent dies down into a slumber,
So die the waves, the lightning and thunder.

Olivia Bentley (10)
Thomas's Kensington

Monster City

Welcome to my land - Monster City,
Where the residents are all busy,
This is a land full of dreams,
As the sun smiles sunbeams.

My unruly orange hair like flames blazing around my head,
My mouth becomes a tiny rosebud if somebody makes me red,
My work is a piece of cake, even though it is stupendously silly,
This is me - a beautiful monster - Mr Billy.

I'm a zombie-zapper fighter,
My slimy slug is such a biter,
He bites you, then you go *kaboom!*
You meet your doom.

My colleagues are shining bright,
The sun stares down with its light,
Scatching my bum to think before I get it right,
It's past your bedtime, goodnight!

Luqman Ibrahim (10)
Tiverton Primary School

YOUNG WRITERS INFORMATION

We hope you have enjoyed reading this book – and that you will continue to in the coming years.

If you're a young writer who enjoys reading and creative writing, or the parent of an enthusiastic poet or story writer, do visit our website **www.youngwriters.co.uk**. Here you will find free competitions, workshops and games, as well as recommended reads, a poetry glossary and our blog.

If you would like to order further copies of this book, or any of our other titles, then please give us a call or visit **www.youngwriters.co.uk**.

Young Writers
Remus House
Coltsfoot Drive
Peterborough
PE2 9BF
(01733) 890066
info@youngwriters.co.uk